POETRY MATTERS

Edited By Donna Samworth

First published in Great Britain in 2022 by:

Young Writers
Remus House
Coltsfoot Drive
Peterborough
PE2 9BF
Telephone: 01733 890066
Website: www.youngwriters.co.uk

All Rights Reserved
Book Design by Ashley Janson
© Copyright Contributors 2021
Softback ISBN 978-1-80015-723-1

Printed and bound in the UK by BookPrintingUK
Website: www.bookprintinguk.com
YB0491J

FOREWORD

For Young Writers' latest competition This Is Me, we asked primary school pupils to look inside themselves, to think about what makes them unique, and then write a poem about it! They rose to the challenge magnificently and the result is this fantastic collection of poems in a variety of poetic styles.

Here at Young Writers our aim is to encourage creativity in children and to inspire a love of the written word, so it's great to get such an amazing response, with some absolutely fantastic poems. It's important for children to focus on and celebrate themselves and this competition allowed them to write freely and honestly, celebrating what makes them great, expressing their hopes and fears, or simply writing about their favourite things. This Is Me gave them the power of words. The result is a collection of inspirational and moving poems that also showcase their creativity and writing ability.

I'd like to congratulate all the young poets in this anthology, I hope this inspires them to continue with their creative writing.

CONTENTS

Greensted Junior School, Basildon

Sadie Nina Kemp (9)	1
Abigail Ogundare (9)	2
Rosie George (9)	3
Esme John (7)	4
Harrison Lynch (8)	5
Jamie Luis Duck (7)	6
Alice Matthewman (7)	7
Jessica Taylor (9)	8
Sophie Price (7)	9
Oliver Banham (7)	10
Naomi Imona (7)	11
Megan Watson (9)	12
Daisy Thomas (10)	13
Maddison Lynch (8)	14
Joshua Ogundare (7)	15
Arise Kironde (7)	16
Eliza Compton (11)	17
India Cox (9)	18

Lyndon Green Junior School, Birmingham

Yousaf Nadeem (9)	19
Eesha Choudhury (8)	20
Leo Howell (8)	22
Isha Rehman (8)	24
Fayzan Mohammad (9)	25
Harrison Willett (9)	26
Isabel van Bokhorst (8)	28
Betsy Read (8)	29
Ethan Harker (8)	30
Sara Sadki (9)	31
Jorja McCatcheon (8)	32

Myesha Haroon (8)	33
Muhammad Ubaydullah Hussain (8)	34
Beau Storey (9)	35
Maxen Clark (8)	36
Rudy Seery (8)	37
Kyle Bassi (9)	38
Hurr Mirza (8)	39
Maison Ward (8)	40
Rayyan Aslam (8)	41
Sebastian Male (8)	42
Marques M S Ngoshi (9)	43
Areeb Hasnat (8)	44
Eren Yalcin (9)	45
Mohammed Shayan Miah (8)	46
Zachary Josephs (8)	47
Sofiya Ahmed (8)	48
Teddy Begley (9)	49
Scarlet Taylor (9)	50
Alexander Darnley (8)	51
Lyra Jae Ward (8)	52
Alexander Haria (8)	53
Shahrukh Ahmady (9)	54
Ollie Sanders (8)	55
Safa Jahangir (9)	56
Leo McDade (8)	57
Maya Piekielna (9)	58
Alex Bird (8)	59
Willow Johnston (8)	60
Jack Smith (8)	61
Julian Neilson (8)	62
Ruby Bull (8)	63
Briana Bahica (9)	64
Elsie Cook (9)	65
Martha Morrow (8)	66
Zak Mohammed (8)	67

Mathew Palmer (8)	68
Inayah Rafiq (8)	69
Dexter Williams (8)	70
Thomas Rowley (8)	71
Sienna-Jess Harris (8)	72
Macey Finnegan (8)	73
Oscar-James Pettigrew (8)	74
Indie Knowles (8)	75

Regent House Preparatory School, Newtownards

Erin Gordon (10)	76
Ella van Onselen (9)	77

Southtown Primary School, Southtown

Eva Leal (9)	78
Rory Robbins (9)	80
Cody Milbourn (10)	81
Jamie Ruane (9)	82
Payton Day (9)	83
Beatrix Batista (10)	84
Thiago Boa Morte (10)	85
Junior J Jary (10)	86
Joshua Davies (11)	87
Izabela Rosu (9)	88
Isaac Schepp (9)	89
Gabriela Romao (9)	90
Charlotte Gilham (9)	91
Lilly Clayton (10)	92
Lainie-Mave Wood (7)	93
Sahajpreet Kaur (10)	94
Logan Jonas-Smith (9)	95
Zack Goodwin (10)	96
Lilyane Romao (9)	97
Keegan Ayers (9)	98
Pedro Tavares (9)	99
Darcey Florence Macconnachie (7)	100
Isabelle Stiting (11)	101
Maisie-Jane Fletcher (9)	102
Elise Kirby (7)	103

McKenzie Beer (10)	104
Lillian McKay (11)	105
Lillie-Rose Bacon (10)	106
Viktorija Gumenuka (11)	107
Harry Lunn (10)	108
Madalena De Carvalho (11)	109
William Benjamin (10)	110
Ellison Noel Thompson (7)	111
Andreas Nole	112
Demi-Mai Beer (7)	113
Lila-Star Hunter (7)	114
Freddie Miller (8)	115
Elliot Elijah Prom (8)	116
Caiden Fletcher (7)	117
Jaxon Westgate (10)	118
Lucas Jakus (7)	119

St Charles' Catholic Primary School, Hadfield

Ava Esposito-Maffei (11)	120
Jude Sharpe (10)	121
Natalie Ann Rolls (10)	122
Béa Sues Amore Cassells (10)	123
Amelia Boby (10)	124
Evie Westmerland (10)	125
Maisey Mellor (10)	126
Rosie Thomasson (11)	127
Thomas Doodson (10)	128
Evie Aurora Littler (10)	129
Mabel Mae Margaret Tymon (10)	130
Tomos Wrigglesworth (10)	131
Jessica Bevins (10)	132
Ruby Stilwell (10)	133
Lorenzo Sassanelli (10)	134
Leon Groom (10)	135
Lola Mills (10)	136
Ellie Owen (10)	137

St Theresa's RC School, Finchley

Sophia Varnava (10)	138
Séamus Mac Crossan (10)	141

Evie Keating (10)	142
Darcy O'Donnell (10)	144
Rio Petnga Petnga-Wallace (10)	146
Olivia Dina (10)	148
Mamie Crossan (10)	150
Michal Rojek (10)	152
Lena Rapala (10)	154
Tanisha Chowdhury (10)	155
Connor Balestrini (10)	156
Isabel Luz Martins (10)	157
Ben Blendis (10)	158
Fatima Mohamad (11)	159
Aryo Khoshkam (10)	160
Margaret Rimsa (10)	161
Mikolaj Ceremuga (9)	162
Govind Hariharadas (10)	163
Lily Losi (8)	164
Shirley Suet Ling Chan (9)	165
Jago Hartnett (10)	166
Chimdi Ekezie (11)	167
Arvin	168
Aleksandra Deda (9)	169
Lucas Lazarevic (9)	170
Luke Hare (10)	171
Euan Kirby (10)	172
Nathan Gulati (9)	173
Elizabeth Muci (9)	174
Evie Boverhoff (9)	175
Christina Romanova	176
Lily Farrugia (10)	177
Alice Mariam Subin (8)	178
Alphy Mubiru (11)	179
Erin	180
Gabriella Broom (8)	181
Oliwia Weiss (8)	182
Kristiana Grozdanova (8)	183
Jordan Argiev (10)	184
Dominykas Sapka (10)	185
Sofia Morozova (9)	186
Brendan Amponsah (8)	187
Imina Osaren (9)	188
Nathaniel Asare Yiadom (8)	189
Manuela Maglione (9)	190
Nea Gibson (9)	191
Gabriela Suarez (5)	192
Katy Boverhoff (5)	193
Max S Szymanski (5)	194
Taybah Chowdhury (5)	195
Ted Blendis (5)	196
Elzana Dereje (5)	197

Weavervale Primary School, Frodsham

Honor Anderson (8)	198
Sakhe Ntombela (7)	199
Charlotte Daniels (8)	200
Emeliá-Rose Ellis (7)	201
Noah Winter (8)	202
Daisy Wilson (8)	203
Harriet Hill (7)	204
Lucas Cross (8)	205
Thomas Fairfield (8)	206
Esmai Leicester (7)	207
Matthew Green (8)	208
Lailah Winter (7)	209
Harley Mawdsley (7)	210

THE POEMS

The World Just For Me

There is a world just for me
With beautiful kittens and busy bees
An amazing world for me
With everything I have to have
Plastic cup, beautiful Bella and picnics for me
Chocolate, sweets and food for me!
This is my world, an amazing world for me
Rainbows and unicorns and my cat, Bella, with me
Craziness, madness, nonsense for me!
No responsibilities!
Nice tea and cookies for me!
We ride on the roller coaster of me
Down the emotions, up the feelings
Through the baking, under the making
We are off the roller coaster
This is the world for me.

Sadie Nina Kemp (9)
Greensted Junior School, Basildon

The World Of Me!

If you come into my world, it's never boring.
It's like you're going on a roller-coaster ride, but a crazy one.
If you come into my world, it's never boring.
There's family and laughter inside here.
If you come into my world, it's never boring.
It's Dork Diaries too, and after that experience I'll show you the fun all over again.
If you come into my world, it's never boring.
There's my teacher aka 'one of the best teachers'
I will always love my world.

Abigail Ogundare (9)
Greensted Junior School, Basildon

The Recipe Of Me

A pinch of kindness,
A cup of craziness,
A bowl full of happiness,
A sprinkle of sadness,
Making me is a job,
I am as adventurous as a lion,
I like gymnastics,
A box of curiousness,
I am very bored most of the time,
I feel happy but also sad,
If you see me, you'll be surprised,
I love doing gymnastics,
I am sometimes calm but crazy too,
I would like to be a gymnast,
And yes, hi, this is me, Rosie.

Rosie George (9)
Greensted Junior School, Basildon

This Is Me!

I am smart because I am good at maths.
I am friendly because I like to be kind.
I am good at sport because I like it.
I am kind because I don't like seeing people sad.
I am fun because I like telling jokes.
I am awesome because I always answer correctly.
I am excited when I go somewhere.
I am sometimes happy because I am playing.
I am sometimes curious because I want to know.
I am sometimes messy because I play with toys.

Esme John (7)
Greensted Junior School, Basildon

This Is Me!

I am sporty because I love to play football and other sports.
I am smart because I always get the questions right in maths.
I am kind because I always help people.
I am adventurous because I take it one step at a time and I learn more.
I am happy because I always have a smile on my face.
I am sometimes sad because I have no one to play with.
I am sometimes silly and lazy because I don't do things by myself.

Harrison Lynch (8)
Greensted Junior School, Basildon

This Is Me

I am friendly because I am always kind to everyone.
I am curious all the time because I always want to learn and become the smartest man in existence.
I am sporty because I play a little bit of football but I run around a lot.
I am full of curiosity because I always want to find out things.
I am always ominous when I watch horror films because they scare me.
I am funny because I tell never-ending jokes.

Jamie Luis Duck (7)
Greensted Junior School, Basildon

This Is Me

I have short brown hair
I have brown eyes
I have a loud laugh
I hate to see a fly
Alice has glasses that make her see
If she didn't have them everything would be as small as a bee
Alice is good at dance and likes to sing
If I am sad I like to do a dance
I am very funny and I am crazy
And I always give someone a second chance
I am very messy but sometimes I can be crazy.

Alice Matthewman (7)
Greensted Junior School, Basildon

This Is Who I Am

I am who I want to be,
I love animals and I have two myself,
I love to listen and sing to music,
I wish I could become a famous singer,
People think of me as a girly girl, but I'm not,
I'm as strong as a lion and brave,
I'm a bit of a gamer to be honest,
I'm a big fan of Harry Potter movies,
I love magic and I wish it was real,
That is all about me!

Jessica Taylor (9)
Greensted Junior School, Basildon

This Is Me!

I'm kind because I like to help with friends and I play with my sister.
I'm friendly because I behave and I'm kind to my best, best friend.
I'm awesome because I've got extremely good behaviour.
I'm adventurous because I like to explore the woods.
I'm smart because I'm always interested in work.
I'm always excited because I like to try new things.

Sophie Price (7)
Greensted Junior School, Basildon

This Is Me!

I have short brown hair
I have brown eyes with a tint of yellow
I have legs that run fast
When I see people I know, I always say, "Hello."
I used to be quite shy
I'm good at being silly
I have big wavy arms
But me and Brook are both silly billys
My feet are a bit smelly
I have caramelly eyes
I have a loud laugh
And try to win every prize.

Oliver Banham (7)
Greensted Junior School, Basildon

This Is Me

I am super friendly because I love making new friends.
I am absolutely passionate about following my dreams.
I am fun because I am fun to be around, and I inherited some of the joy from my big sister.
I am fearless because I am not easily scared.
I am adventurous because I love adventures.
I am flexible because I do flexibility routines every week, so that has helped me a lot.

Naomi Imona (7)
Greensted Junior School, Basildon

My Recipe

First of all, a jug of happiness,
Next, a bucket of kindness,
People think I'm weak but I will add strength!
Of course, a load of gaming,
A tiny pinch of lazy into the pot,
I am caring to absolutely everyone, so add that,
One hundred per cent of a jug of dancer and singer,
Five buckets of Stitch and Harry Potter,
In the oven for nine years, and you have me!

Megan Watson (9)
Greensted Junior School, Basildon

All About Me!

U seful, united and helpful
N ice person you can always count on
I ncredible, brave and smart
Q uiet as a mouse, but bright with my friends
U ndeniably talented
E xcellent at drawing and dancing
N ever negative and always happy
E nergetic and bubbly
S weet like honey
S uccessful and hard-working.

Daisy Thomas (10)
Greensted Junior School, Basildon

This Is Me!

Sometimes I am a bit excited, then very crazy.
I am smart with loads of knowledge, but sometimes I get a bit worried.
I am friendly, but angry with some people sometimes.
I am adventurous because I look for balls with my brother because he hides them everywhere in the house.
Sometimes I can be a bit messy, but I don't worry because everyone has a messy room sometimes.

Maddison Lynch (8)
Greensted Junior School, Basildon

This Is Me

I have short black hair
I have a funny flair.
I love cartoons
Especially Looney Tunes.
I try to have sensitive humour
But I love to laugh with pride.
I am a gamer on my Switch
I love to cheat, all I do is pinch my brother.
I'm very crazy
I act like a daisy.
I'm very sporty
I like to run forty metres.

Joshua Ogundare (7)
Greensted Junior School, Basildon

This Is Me!

I am good at maths because I improve my work.
I am smart because I know all about doctors.
I am flexible because I love doing gymnastics and I do it with my best friend.
I am helpful because when children fall over I help them and tell the teacher.
I am friendly because when someone needs help, I do it straight away.

Arise Kironde (7)
Greensted Junior School, Basildon

All About Me

A lways ready for any action and an adventure!
R estless from thinking and constantly learning.
T all, thoughtful, tough.
I ntelligent with a funny side.
S ilent when I'm thinking but not when I chat.
T hank you for listening to my poem about me.

Eliza Compton (11)
Greensted Junior School, Basildon

All About Me

This is all about me,
It's like a never-ending story
Of an incredible life,
It's full of fun and happiness.
It's like a cool life cycle but even better than that,
It's like a funfair that never ends.
It has everything I need in it,
My family and friends.

India Cox (9)
Greensted Junior School, Basildon

This Is Me

Awesome, incredible, I'm dramatic, I make jokes
Football is my superpower
But when I go to school I get grumpy in the morning
This is me!

I'm angry sometimes and happy
I get extremely hyper sometimes
I am funny and friendly
I love spending money
This is me!

I like video games and I like basketball
I'm very crazy sometimes, and adventurous
I am chilled and like running
I get annoyed by my big brother
This is me!

I get very brave sometimes
I'm messy, impatient
I like watching TV and like playing games
Sometimes I'm in a bad mood, I get very bad
This is me!

Yousaf Nadeem (9)
Lyndon Green Junior School, Birmingham

This Is Me!

Enjoyable, nice
I'm sometimes sad
But my brother always makes me mad
This is me!

I'm nice, I'm lonely
I'm brave, I'm good
I love fast food
I can go on my iPad whenever I can
This is me!

I'm bored at home but I find something to do
I can be jolly and a freak
Sometimes I'm crazy
My work can be difficult
I can be happy and funny
This is me!

I have good days
My mum home cooks
I get mad because I get bored
Then I don't like going to bed

I'm lonely because no one wants to play with me
This is me!

Eesha Choudhury (8)
Lyndon Green Junior School, Birmingham

This Is Me!

Gamer genius
Adventurous and cheeky
I love football and video games
I like to read and feed pets
This is me!

I'm always laughing and farting and darting
I love to slide about
I like to spy on my mom
This is me!

I play football, I'm a keeper
I try my best
I'm sneaking into space
This is me!

Always eating chocolate and sweets
I play with my mates sometimes, it's carnage!
I also play in the field
This is me!

I like crystals, gems and diamonds
Milkshakes are my favourite
I hate mushrooms though
This is me!

Leo Howell (8)
Lyndon Green Junior School, Birmingham

This Is Me!

Optimistic, kind
Sometimes late at night I stare at the lamp light
My mind starts running away and I start thinking about my day
This is me!

Being born an only child my thoughts run wild
I think about my pet birds, who although speak no words
Make me feel happy because they always act a little wacky
This is me!

The birds make me laugh loudly and make me want to hold them proudly
I give them their favourite seed which is a part of their daily need
In the morning they start their chirping and I find myself burping
This is me!

Isha Rehman (8)
Lyndon Green Junior School, Birmingham

This Is Me!

Funny, fantastic,
With a mind-blowing brain,
Maths is my speciality,
But I hate it when I cannot play,
This is me!
I'm fearless, I'm friendly,
I love playing games,
A lifelong football fan,
I play with my cousin whenever I can,
This is me!
I'm awesome, I'm amazing,
I can be bored or happy,
Sometimes I can go crazy,
Sometimes I can be calm,
This is me!
I have happy and boring days,
I rarely go outside,
The rain is brought to an end,
Then I can go outside,
This is me!

Fayzan Mohammad (9)
Lyndon Green Junior School, Birmingham

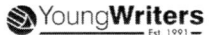

This Is Me!

Fast and fierce
Bold and brave
Super and speedy
Intelligent and intellectual
This is me!

Caring and daring
Thoughtful and thrilling
Brainy and brilliant
Amazingly awesome
This is me!

Exceptionally astounding
Always ecstatic
This is me!

Confident and cool
Super scientific
Sporty and sly
Super and sharing
This is me!

A kind mind
Football, tennis and runs
Are what I do for fun
Happy and sometimes even batty
This is me!

Harrison Willett (9)
Lyndon Green Junior School, Birmingham

This Is Me!

Sweet, elegant
A classy, happy girl
I love food, art is my superpower
This is me!

When I have to go somewhere I get excited
I dance, I fall, I get back up
I'm very strong when it comes to playing
This is me!

I love fast food, I like to spin
I know I will get dizzy
I like a little grub at night
This is me!

I'm very funny, make people laugh
I have good friends, they are very kind
I'm a cute girl
This is me!

Isabel van Bokhorst (8)
Lyndon Green Junior School, Birmingham

This Is Me!

Brilliant, hyper,
I'm sometimes bonkers,
Gymnastics is my superpower,
But I hate getting out of bed,
This is me!
I'm funny, I like pocket money,
I hate heights,
I like to bite food,
I'm sweet like honey,
This is me!
I'm a good friend,
I have a best bud,
I love the mud,
But I always get messy,
This is me!
I love maths,
I don't like baths,
I love to practise for gym,
But I hate bins,
This is me!

Betsy Read (8)
Lyndon Green Junior School, Birmingham

This Is Me!

I'm sometimes brainy
And really gamey
Crafty and sneaky
Sporty and speedy
This is me!

I'm very sly
And I also like to spy
I like to run
Because I do it for fun
This is me!

I'm really scientific
And fierce and furious
I am very clean
And sometimes tidy
This is me!

I'm very confident
And really kind
And always helpful
And sometimes cheeky
This is me!

Ethan Harker (8)
Lyndon Green Junior School, Birmingham

This Is Me!

Funny and with vim
And very, very prim
With a little drop
I'm a shining star!
This is me!

I love gymnastics
And I'm the type!
Love to learn
And love fun!
This is me!

Gracious and with vim
Tidy and prim
Shy and sly
Family-friendly
This is me!

Confident with a confused mind
Generous and kind
With a creative mind!
I rate my family highly!
This is me!

Sara Sadki (9)
Lyndon Green Junior School, Birmingham

This Is Me!

Kind, joyful
I'm my own person
I love horses
Dancing and singing is my superpower
But my little sister is sometimes a bit annoying
This is me!

I am a secret dancer
I love hanging with a big group of friends
I am kind, I am funny, I spend a lot of money
This is me!

I love creating things
I would love to be a famous artist someday, it is my dream
I love hopping like a bunny
This is me!

Jorja McCatcheon (8)
Lyndon Green Junior School, Birmingham

This Is Me

I am neat and I love treats
I'm average and alarming, also hardworking
I'm crafty and very snatchy and also lazy
This is me!

I am frightened of spiders and also liars
I am forgetful and kind and really, really nice!
I help people when they cry or get hurt
This is me!

I am joyful and blessed and I'm really, really fresh
I am interested in sharks with their really big marks
This is me!

Myesha Haroon (8)
Lyndon Green Junior School, Birmingham

This Is Me

I'm funny, generous and kind
My maths skills will blow your mind
This is me!
I like to cook, but I need the recipe book
In my spare time I ride my bike
But I've got to be careful in case my brother strikes.
This is me!
When the sky is nice and bright I help my brother fly his kite
I'm a good role model to my little brother
That sure impresses my mother
This is me!

Muhammad Ubaydullah Hussain (8)
Lyndon Green Junior School, Birmingham

This Is Me!

Curious, adventurous,
I'm sometimes silly,
But also mature,
Horse riding is my superpower,
This is me!
I walk, I trot, I canter,
At horse riding,
I'm merry but I worry a lot,
This is me!
I'm kind,
I've got an intelligent mind,
My friends make me happy but,
When I'm tired,
I turn into a mouse,
All quiet,
This is me!

Beau Storey (9)
Lyndon Green Junior School, Birmingham

This Is Me!

I'm smart, happy,
I'm a star at maths,
Karate is my superpower,
I'm a fantastic bookworm,
This is me!
I'm a positive mind,
But I have marvellous speed,
When a teacher is cruel I get hot,
This is me!
I'm mad,
I'm sad,
Though I'm a lad,
This is me!
I love playing games,
I'm eight years old,
This is me!

Maxen Clark (8)
Lyndon Green Junior School, Birmingham

This Is Me!

Silly and kind, energetic and thoughtful
With a scientific mind, messy and smiley
This is me!

Bold and fearless, sporty and smart
Passionate and happy
This is me!

Cheeky and sometimes angry
Sad and glad, funny and clumsy
This is me!

Friends and family are always fun
Chocolates and sweets, I love animals and treats
This is me!

Rudy Seery (8)
Lyndon Green Junior School, Birmingham

This Is Me!

Sleepy and cheeky
Funny and sneaky
Caring and loving
Gleaming and chatty
This is me!

Football and tennis are
What I do for fun
Angry and silly
Chaotic and confident
This is me!

Messy and pleasant
Brainy and smart
Sweet, lovely and sharing
Sassy and always cheesed off
This is me!

Kyle Bassi (9)
Lyndon Green Junior School, Birmingham

This Is Me!

Loyal, brave, I'm generous,
And I care about others,
I'm kind to my parents,
This is me.

I'm creative, I'm strong,
I'm not good at every game,
This is me.

I'm intelligent and I like to read.
I don't like people who make fun of me,
My superpower is dodgeball,
This is me.

Hurr Mirza (8)
Lyndon Green Junior School, Birmingham

This Is Me

Strong, handsome
I'm sometimes mad
My superpower is football
But I hurt myself
This is me!

I hurt myself
I like rabbits, I hop
Like when I run
I jump, I play football
This is me!

I like the zoo
I like my sports
I wish to be a professional
Footballer like Messi
This is me!

Maison Ward (8)
Lyndon Green Junior School, Birmingham

This Is Me!

I'm really funny,
I hop like a bunny,
I love spending money,
I love kicking dummies,
This is me!
I'm awesome,
My name is not Lawson,
I wasn't born in autumn,
I'm really important,
This is me!
I'm smart,
I'm talented,
I'm tiny,
But I'm not spiky,
This is me!

Rayyan Aslam (8)
Lyndon Green Junior School, Birmingham

This Is Me

I am kind, brave and write rhymes,
I love sharks, I love going to the park,
I have a superpower, karate,
I love autumn but I was not born in autumn,
I love food,
I want to be a hero,
I am a good gamer,
I can cook a little bit,
This is me!

I am really good at Minecraft,
I love YouTube,
This is me!

Sebastian Male (8)
Lyndon Green Junior School, Birmingham

This Is Me

I am merry like a cherry tree when Santa says,
"Merry Christmas!" to a mouse named Jerry
My superpower is being clever
This is me!

I help my little brother with maths and times tables
This is me!

I'm fearful and tall
I'm nearly the size of a board, no one can match my size
This is me!

Marques M S Ngoshi (9)
Lyndon Green Junior School, Birmingham

This Is Me!

Caring and daring
Glorious and sharing
Shifty and curious
Bright and ecstatic
This is me!

Intellectual and smart
Fast like a dart
Smiley and cheerful
I rate my friends highly
This is me!

Impatient and kind
Joyful and messy
Sometimes funny
Eager and joyful
This is me!

Areeb Hasnat (8)
Lyndon Green Junior School, Birmingham

This Is Me!

Strong and caring
Sneaky and daring
Running and jumping
And always talking
This is me!

Happy and laughing
Cheeky and sometimes rude
Smart and cool
Always in a good mood
This is me!

Football and tennis are how I have fun
Kicking and serving
I always do my best
This is me!

Eren Yalcin (9)
Lyndon Green Junior School, Birmingham

This Is Me!

Pleasant and kind
With a creative mind
Tidy and clean
Happy and smiley
This is me!

Jumping and sporty
Sharing and caring
Shy and quiet
Cheeky and sneaky
This is me!

Crisps and chocolates
Joking and funny
Confident and smart
Unafraid and strong
This is me!

Mohammed Shayan Miah (8)
Lyndon Green Junior School, Birmingham

This Is Me!

Awesome and helpful
Positive and sensible
Smart and funny
Happy and smiley
This is me!

Funny and messy
Cheeky and sneaky
This is me!

Nervous and shy
Bold and fierce
Grumpy and angry
This is me!

Kind and smart
Positive and friendly
This is me!

Zachary Josephs (8)
Lyndon Green Junior School, Birmingham

This Is Me!

S lime, I love playing with slime and poking slime
O ctober is my mum's sister's birthday
F ashionable are my dolls, and babies and stories
I like it when I go to Latvia
Y ay, I have clay and squishes and my iPad
A nd I like playing Tower of Hell and Roblox.

Sofiya Ahmed (8)
Lyndon Green Junior School, Birmingham

This Is Me!

My name is Teddy
But people call me Ted,
I'm always in my comfy bed,
Like I said, my name is Ted.

This is me!
I saw a book and I thought,
That looks good, but my friend said,
"Oh no, no, no, that book is bad and sad,"
So I thought it would make me mad.

Teddy Begley (9)
Lyndon Green Junior School, Birmingham

This Is Me!

Sassy and bold
Kind and caring
Cheeky and fashionable
Sharing and caring
This is me!
Friendly and bright
Joyful and bold
Clean and organised
Helpful and nice
This is me!
Dancing and singing
What I do for fun
Creative mind
Lovely and kind
This is me!

Scarlet Taylor (9)
Lyndon Green Junior School, Birmingham

This Is Me!

Fast and fearless
Silly and cheeky
Loud but friendly
Chatty and laughing
This is me!

Football and basketball
Are the sports I love
Holidays and sandy beaches
Are what I like and do for fun
This is me!

Always hungry
Smiley and happy
This is me!

Alexander Darnley (8)
Lyndon Green Junior School, Birmingham

This Is Me

I'm curious, I'm sleepy
But I'm not so cheeky
I'm messy and I'm not tall
But you will not make me stop liking football
This is me!

I'm passionate and playful
Cheeky and cheerful
I'm very cool
And I play with footballs
This is me!

Lyra Jae Ward (8)
Lyndon Green Junior School, Birmingham

This Is Me!

  A mazing at sport
  L ove basketball
  E nergetic all the time
e **X** tremely great at times tables
  A ctive and cool
  N othing I am scared of
  D ominating games
  E xcellent and clever
  R eally love action. This is me!

Alexander Haria (8)
Lyndon Green Junior School, Birmingham

This Is Me!

Nice, brave,
Sometimes bad at listening,
Running is my superpower,
But early mornings make me cower,
I like talking, laughing,
I can be crazy or chilled,
I make violence or sometimes I am silent,
I have bad days when I get hurt,
I rarely have bad moods.

Shahrukh Ahmady (9)
Lyndon Green Junior School, Birmingham

This Is Me!

I'm polite
I'm mostly a delight
But if you take my food
I will be in a bad mood
This is me!

I like phones
And I've never broken my bones
I'm fearless and I'm curious
And I will be victorious
This is me!

Ollie Sanders (8)
Lyndon Green Junior School, Birmingham

This Is Me!

Intelligent and silly
Pretty and sassy
Positive and fun
I love playing in the sun
This is me!

Happy and daring
Loving and caring
Dancey and giggly
Sleepy and cheeky
And sometimes geeky
This is me!

Safa Jahangir (9)
Lyndon Green Junior School, Birmingham

This Is Me!

I like to party
And eat pizza
Faster than a cheetah
I will be pleased to meet ya
This is me!

As intelligent as Einstein
Super sporty and tall
Me and Subhan are cool
We also adore football
This is me!

Leo McDade (8)
Lyndon Green Junior School, Birmingham

This Is Me

I'm a wonderful girl
I have beautiful hair
I'm tall and kind
With a clever mind
This is me!
I'm helpful and active
But sometimes angry
I love to do tap
And the audience claps
This is me!

Maya Piekielna (9)
Lyndon Green Junior School, Birmingham

This Is Me!

I like watching TV
I love playing with my dogs
I love eating anything
But okay
This is me!

I play Super Smash Bros.
I like my Nintendo
I enjoy nature
And my name is Alex
This is me!

Alex Bird (8)
Lyndon Green Junior School, Birmingham

This Is Me!

Loyal and kind
With a creative mind
Sweet and cool
I love a game of pool
This is me!

Sneaky and sleepy
And sometimes even cheeky
Speedy and super
And amazingly awesome
This is me!

Willow Johnston (8)
Lyndon Green Junior School, Birmingham

This Is Me

I'm blissful, playful,
Sometimes I jump around,
I'm sad,
My superpower is football,
And I like playing
With my dad and sister,
And I like swimming,
Sometimes my sister is annoying.

Jack Smith (8)
Lyndon Green Junior School, Birmingham

This Is Me!

I like 4M
It's a wonderful class
I'm having a ball
And I'm extremely tall
This is me!

I like Mathew
But not mats
I like maths
But not tricky maths
This is me!

Julian Neilson (8)
Lyndon Green Junior School, Birmingham

This Is Me!

I am kind, I am wonderful and I am fun
And I eat scrumptious food and watch TV
This is me!

I am hot and pretty
I am lovely and smart
I am helpful and I help the teacher
This is me!

Ruby Bull (8)
Lyndon Green Junior School, Birmingham

This Is Me!

B eautiful and kind
R espectful and generous
I ncredible and sweet
A mazing and wonderful
N ew to this school
A nd I'm incredibly tall. This is me!

Briana Bahica (9)
Lyndon Green Junior School, Birmingham

This Is Me!

Clever and kind
Friendly and fun
I'm really messy
And I love cooking
This is me!

Sleepy and cool
I love eating
And watching TV
I'm so cool
This is me!

Elsie Cook (9)
Lyndon Green Junior School, Birmingham

This Is Me!

M oody and marvellous
A crobatic and awesome
R espectful and responsible
T iny as a mouse
H ungry at lunchtimes
A wesome at school. This is me!

Martha Morrow (8)
Lyndon Green Junior School, Birmingham

This Is Me!

I'm a director
I'm a rich kid
I have a daily run
I'm bold and brave
This is me!

I am strong
I am cool
I am in school
I am fast
This is me!

Zak Mohammed (8)
Lyndon Green Junior School, Birmingham

This Is Me!

M arvellous man
A wesome and amazing
T all and cool
H as a hairy dad
E xtraordinary and excellent
W onderful and wicked. This is me.

Mathew Palmer (8)
Lyndon Green Junior School, Birmingham

This Is Me!

I ntelligent and incredible
N ervous but excited
A wesome and amazing
Y outhful and sweet
A ctive and creative
H umble and helpful.

Inayah Rafiq (8)
Lyndon Green Junior School, Birmingham

This Is Me!

D on't give up
E at all of my dinner
X for x in Dexter
T alking and chatting
E veryone likes me
R ed is my favourite colour.

Dexter Williams (8)
Lyndon Green Junior School, Birmingham

This Is Me!

T hinking like a genius
H andsome and brave
O rganised
M ythical Beast Quest
A mazing boy
S uper cool. This is me.

Thomas Rowley (8)
Lyndon Green Junior School, Birmingham

This Is Me!

S illy and funny
I 'm a fear
E ating my fruit
N ever naughty!
N ever mean
A lways helpful and kind.

Sienna-Jess Harris (8)
Lyndon Green Junior School, Birmingham

This Is Me!

Playing and laughing
Is how I have fun
I'm very kind and I have a creative mind
Caring and adventurous
I always do my best
This is me!

Macey Finnegan (8)
Lyndon Green Junior School, Birmingham

This Is Me

O cean loving
S kateboarding
C lever at video games
A dventurous
R iding my scooter is my favourite thing to do.

Oscar-James Pettigrew (8)
Lyndon Green Junior School, Birmingham

This Is Me!

I am snazzy and jazzy
N ice and happy
D aring and sharing
I ndie is a joyful girl
E xcited about school.

Indie Knowles (8)
Lyndon Green Junior School, Birmingham

My Life

T iny puppies are one of my favourite things.
H orse riding is one of my passions.
I love to bake, yum-yum when the oven pings.
S eeing Skye vs Star in a competition, Skye has a better sense of fashion.

I 'm very intelligent at it all.
S chool is an absolute ball.

M e, well I like swimming and pony riding.
E rin is my name, in school I use adding and dividing.

Erin Gordon (10)
Regent House Preparatory School, Newtownards

The Way I Live

T ime to play and read.
H appiness with kittens.
E lla is my name.

W ork is organised.
A lexandria is my sister.
Y o-yos and fun games.

I 'm very grateful.

L ove my family.
I nside my treehouse.
V entures in my garden.
E veryone is friends.

Ella van Onselen (9)
Regent House Preparatory School, Newtownards

This Is Me

A recipe to make me
You will need:
A little sift of calm
Cute babies
A chop of friends
A knead of craziness
A jug o' singing
A slice of cheesy pizza
A sprinkle of sleepovers
A dash of creativity
A sprinkle of a warm bedroom
A blob of family

Method:
First, sift a little calm into a bowl, with a dash of cute babies
Then, add a dash of creativity
After that, pour a dash of friend and craziness into a bowl
Then add a chop of a cheesy pizza and singing
Then a sprinkle of sleepover and a warm bedroom

Add a big blob of family
Then have a mix and leave it to cool and I am there.

Eva Leal (9)
Southtown Primary School, Southtown

A Recipe To Make Me

A cup of lovely digestives and great tea
A slice of World War II
With a pinch of Spitfires
Also a dash of T-34s
And a sprinkle of enemy soldiers
A spoonful of friends, animals and family
A dollop of guns

Method:
Now, you need to take the slice of World War II.
Then add the pinch of Spitfires.
After that you need to put the dash of T-34s on top.
Then sprinkle the enemy soldiers on the sides.
Add the spoonful of friends, animals and family with the dash of T-34s.
Then mix the digestives and tea into it.
Then add a dollop of guns.
Put it into the oven then boom, you're done.

Rory Robbins (9)
Southtown Primary School, Southtown

A Recipe To Create Me

You will need:
An enormous room filled with PS5s
A cup of green, fizzy sherbet crystals
A dash of creativity
A football stud that gives you the best grip in the world
A slice of an Arsenal ticket
A sprinkle of short temper

Now you need to:
First, pour the cup of green, fizzy sherbet crystals
After, mix it in with the football stud
Next, add the enormous room filled with PS5s
Then, put in a slice of an Arsenal ticket
After that, put it in the oven
Finally, wait for it to set and add a dash of creativity, and a sprinkle of short temper.

Cody Milbourn (10)
Southtown Primary School, Southtown

This Is Me, Jamie

T all in size.
H is friends are the best.
I am trustworthy and independent unless people need my help.
S o I'm nice and helpful.

I love my pup.
S o generous. The FBI is crazy.

M e, yes, me. I love PE.
E ven I like a spooky month (FNAF).

J amie likes Brazil.
A nd I am very good at games.
M y dog is like a friend.
I love red pandas.
E ven I know how to cook.

Jamie Ruane (9)
Southtown Primary School, Southtown

This Is Me

A recipe to make me
You will need:
A cupful of kindness
A dash of cats' tails
A slice of friends
A spoonful of art
A sprinkle of happiness
A pinch of fun
One kilogram of paintings
The feel of a roller coaster.

Method:
First, add a slice of friends
Next, add a cupful of kindness
Then, add a dash of cats' tails
Now, blend in one kilogram of paintings
After that, sprinkle in the feeling of a roller coaster.

Payton Day (9)
Southtown Primary School, Southtown

This Is Me!

If I were an animal
A cheetah I would be
So I could run really fast
And bite people if they abused me.

If I were a fruit
A watermelon I would be
So I could be fresh
And roll away from the bowl.

If I were a colour
Blue I would be
So I could be bright
And shine like the sky.

If I were a musical instrument
A keyboard I would be
So I could be calm
And play relaxing music.

Beatrix Batista (10)
Southtown Primary School, Southtown

This Is Me

If I were a fruit
A strawberry I would be
As red is my favourite colour.

If I were an animal
A lion I would be
As the lion is one of the strongest animals.

If I were an insect
A spider I would be
As it can scare people.

If I were an object
A chair I would be
As it can't be destroyed so easily.

If I were a colour
Red I would be
As it's my favourite colour.

Thiago Boa Morte (10)
Southtown Primary School, Southtown

This Is Me

  J oy is within me
  U nique I can be
  N ormal as I can be
  I am as simple as I can be
  O bsessed with Xbox
  R eally good at games I am.

I like my Xbox
I have blonde hair, blue eyes
I am a midget
I have a big mouth, small ears, small eyes
I love games, family, friends, Pokémon cards
I have two dogs, one cat and fish
I have six sisters, two mums, two dads.

Junior J Jary (10)
Southtown Primary School, Southtown

This Is Me!

J oking like the Joker from Batman
O verpowered, but I'm not really
S illy all the time
H appy when people are nice
U nusual, I am very unusual
A nnoying but only sometimes!

D ream is to be the best Minecraft player
A mazing of course
V ery artistic
I ndependent in all my work
E legant in my own way
S paghetti! I love it.

Joshua Davies (11)
Southtown Primary School, Southtown

A Recipe To Make Me

To create me, you'll need:
A spoonful of happiness
A cup of shopping
Three cups of joy
A sprinkle of family
Two spoons of school
A dollop of adventures
And half a cup of creativity.

Method:
First, whisk up the full spoon of happiness with half a cup of creativity
Second, knead the adventures and add them all together
Put it in the oven, let it sit
Take it out and sprinkle with family.

Izabela Rosu (9)
Southtown Primary School, Southtown

This Is Me

T iny in size
H elpful and kind
I 'm funny and smart
S aving goals in football.

I 'm sometimes naughty
S illy and rude.

M y cat is the best thing ever
E ating food.

I love Australia
S piders are my favourite
A merican is an amazing country
A nd I have nice friends
C ereal tastes good too.

Isaac Schepp (9)
Southtown Primary School, Southtown

Riddle About Me

I like going shopping with my mom
I am funny like my sis, my dad, my mom
I like dancing with my sis, mom and dad
I have three siblings
I like looking after babies
I like looking after pets
I like playing with my pet dog
I love my family
I like riding my bike
I like Lamborghinis
I like watching movies
I like singing
I like having fun
I like maths.

Gabriela Romao (9)
Southtown Primary School, Southtown

This Is Me

C hristmas is my favourite season.
H orses are the animals I like best.
A rt is my favourite subject.
R oblox is the game I love to play.
L iverpool is what my family cheers for.
O ctober is my birthday!
T rustworthy is my thing.
T he love with my family is huge.
E aster is fun because I love treasure hunts.

Charlotte Gilham (9)
Southtown Primary School, Southtown

About Me!

L oving to my family
I ndependent
L unatic outside
L aughing at the silliest things
Y elling at my siblings.

C lever in life
L onely in school
A ngry all the time
Y ellow is a colour I hate
T aller than most people
O rganised in the desk
N ormal! Like everyone else!

Lilly Clayton (10)
Southtown Primary School, Southtown

This Is Me!

I am Lainie-Mave
I am seven
I am in Year 3
I am as kind as a flower.

    L oves hot dogs
    A lways tries to be amazing
    I wish I was a witch
    N ever gives up
    I am independent
    E xcellent

    M ight sometimes get sad
    A lways talks
    V ery silly
    E verybody is my friend.

Lainie-Mave Wood (7)
Southtown Primary School, Southtown

This Is Me!

S ugar is sweet like me
A rt is my favourite lesson
H orses are my friends
A pples are sweet to me
J am is yuck to me
P rincesses are as cool as they can be
R ings are shiny like my cheeks
E ggs are warm to me
E lephants are scary to me
T igers are cute, just like me.

Sahajpreet Kaur (10)
Southtown Primary School, Southtown

To Create Me You Will Need

You will need:
Laces from a football boot
A claw from a claw machine
A slice from an Arsenal shirt
A cup of FIFA giftcard
Half of a golfball

Now you need to:
First, add the laces from a football boot
Next, pour it all into the claw machine
Then, add the golfball and the FIFA giftcard
Finally, put it in the oven.

Logan Jonas-Smith (9)
Southtown Primary School, Southtown

This Is Me!

Z ack is my name
A mazing is my game
C ool as I can be
K arate is me!

G ood at karate I can be
O bsessed with it I like to be
O range belt is my dream
D edicated I am
W illing to be the best I can be
I can be the best
N ot giving up, not for me.

Zack Goodwin (10)
Southtown Primary School, Southtown

Rhyme About Me

I pray to God
I like being with my family
I like shopping with my mom
I like riding my gold and black bike
I like dancing, BLACKPINK
I like music, Rihanna
I like art, sea creatures
I have a big heart
I help people
I like pranking my sisters
I play limbo
I like looking after dogs
I am funny
This is me.

Lilyane Romao (9)
Southtown Primary School, Southtown

My Name Is Keegan

Sometimes mean.
I am as fast as a Tesla.
I am quick in football boots.
Sometimes I am a messer.
I'm stronger than a bear.

My friends are dudes.
Sometimes in a mood.
I have been to four countries.
Just joking, been to more countries.
Like playing video games all day.
Rather do that than go outside to play.

Keegan Ayers (9)
Southtown Primary School, Southtown

This Is Me

My name is Pedro
I love my Lego
I am as fast as a hare
Strong as a bear.

Well, my friends are dudes
Sometimes in a mood
My superpower is maths
But never take a bath
I like DaBaby
But not a baby.

I am sometimes funny
And squeak like a bunny
I love iPhones and iPads
I wear metal shinpads.

Pedro Tavares (9)
Southtown Primary School, Southtown

This Is Me!

D og lover
A nimal carer
R oblox player
C at adorer
E gg hater
Y ellow exposer.

F lower grower
L ion lover
O tter liker
R iver swimmer
E gg head
N ature carer
C hocolate eater
E xcellent at drawing.

Darcey Florence Macconnachie (7)
Southtown Primary School, Southtown

This Is Me!

I ndependent because I can do anything on my own
S illy because I make big messes
A mazing because I am beautiful
B eautiful because I am amazing
E legant, I'm very posh
L iar because sometimes I
L ie and don't tell the truth
E nergy because I like eating sugar.

Isabelle Stiting (11)
Southtown Primary School, Southtown

This Is Me

T he outdoors is my place to be.
H elpful at home and at school.
I love playing with my friends.
S ensitive and sporty.

I am independent and creative.
S inging is my favourite thing to do.

M eerkats are my animal.
E nergetic most of the time.

Maisie-Jane Fletcher (9)
Southtown Primary School, Southtown

This Is Me

E xcellent at maths
L oves McDonald's Happy Meals
I ntelligent
S pace is so fascinating
E xcited.

K FC is so tasty
I nventor is what I want to be
R eads interesting books
B urger King makes me happy
Y ouTube lover.

Elise Kirby (7)
Southtown Primary School, Southtown

This Is Me

M ajestic boy I can be
C ool as cola I try to be
K angaroos I'd like to see
E xcellent teachers I have to help me
N octurnal animals I always see
Z zz all the time
I ndividual youngsters have to rhyme
E xperiments are what I like.

McKenzie Beer (10)
Southtown Primary School, Southtown

All About Me
Haiku poetry

I enjoy pasta
It is my favourite food
And biscuits are too!

I enjoy reading
School is fun and exciting
Maths is amazing.

I have two cute pets
A rabbit called Timothy
And Rosie the dog.

I am very kind
I believe I am helpful
And very honest.

Lillian McKay (11)
Southtown Primary School, Southtown

This Is Me

I like my pets, they're like family to me
Gaming is my thing, Minecraft and Fortnite are the best
My hobbies are football, ballet and reading
I'm a kind, caring, sweet and innocent girl
I love animals, bunnies are great but my pets are more special than strays
Strays are great.

Lillie-Rose Bacon (10)
Southtown Primary School, Southtown

Acrostic Poem

V iktorija is my name
I ntelligent is what I am
K ind I really am
T eam, I'm a good teammate
O rganised I am
R eading is my favourite
I magination, I'm good at it
J oyful, I always smile
A ngel from Heaven.

Viktorija Gumenuka (11)
Southtown Primary School, Southtown

This Is Me!

H elpful to my family
A great younger brother
R ich with love
R espectful to animals
Y oung and energetic.

L ove my family
U nique!
N ice with friends
N ever drink orange juice.

Harry Lunn (10)
Southtown Primary School, Southtown

Me!

I'm a daydreaming person
But my day can worsen
Mischievously smart
With a very kind heart
I never give up
And have amazingly good luck
Never change yourself
Even if you break apart
And start your day
In a very good way.

Madalena De Carvalho (11)
Southtown Primary School, Southtown

This Is Me

I am very kind
I play Fortnite with my friends
I have a lot of friends.

I like my school lots
The school work is very easy
The school is funny.

My nan was a cook
I love electric keyboards
I play NFL.

William Benjamin (10)
Southtown Primary School, Southtown

This Is Ellison

I like doing karate
I love games
I like doing sports
My dream job is wrestling
My hero is Ultimate Warrior
My favourite band is Queen
My favourite song is Seven Seas of Rhye
My favourite food is a cheeseburger.

Ellison Noel Thompson (7)
Southtown Primary School, Southtown

This Is Me!

A great football player
N o dog for me
D ad is like a lion to me
R uns fast
E ats lots of chocolate
A lways serious in the classroom
S mart and funny.

Andreas Nole
Southtown Primary School, Southtown

Demi-Mai

D elightful dancer
E at scrambled eggs
M aths is great
I love my family

M cDonald's is my favourite
A lways working hard
I like literacy.

Demi-Mai Beer (7)
Southtown Primary School, Southtown

This Is Me!

L ovely
I ncredible at reading
L ove McDonald's Happy Meals
A mazing friend

S uper kind
T igers are cool
A nimal lover
R oblox.

Lila-Star Hunter (7)
Southtown Primary School, Southtown

This Is Me

F ootballer
R eady for pizza
E xcellent at maths
D ribbles like Neymar
D apper shooter
I magining winning a tournament
E njoys YouTube.

Freddie Miller (8)
Southtown Primary School, Southtown

This Is Me

E xcellent at reading
L oving person
L ove my perfect sisters and brothers
I ncredible
O utstanding at riding my bike
T all for my age.

Elliot Elijah Prom (8)
Southtown Primary School, Southtown

This Is Me!

C ool
A m extremely good at karate
I ncredible and intelligent
D og lover
E xcellent at riding my bike
N ever misbehaves.

Caiden Fletcher (7)
Southtown Primary School, Southtown

Jaxon

J axon is my name
A ttractive young boy
X ylophones, I want to play them
O utstanding at football
N ature-loving boy.

Jaxon Westgate (10)
Southtown Primary School, Southtown

This Is Me!

L egendary at Minecraft
U ltimate Jurassic World player
C ollects dinosaur toys
A lways helping others
S uper smart.

Lucas Jakus (7)
Southtown Primary School, Southtown

This Is Me!

Flying across the court, the netball was on fire,
Dancing away, the netball laughed,
I had my chance to shoot, it went in, the net burst into fierce flames,
My favourite sport is netball.

Boing! went the new taste in my mouth,
Wham, the idea hit me like a cannonball,
I love trying new things,
I like experimenting like a mad scientist.

My dog ran across the field as fast as a car,
My dog is called Max,
Max is as cuddly as a teddy bear,
Like a bullet, Max darted towards the squirrel.

The aeroplane flies in the sky like a bird,
The security searched the suitcase like a hawk,
Like a crocodile catching its prey, the suitcase closed,
I like to travel.

Ava Esposito-Maffei (11)
St Charles' Catholic Primary School, Hadfield

This Is Me

I am caring, I am kind, I think in a nice state of mind,
Now this begs the question to the riddle, who is this?
And who am I? I like football: penalty!
I'll give you a clue: it represents me,
Who is writing this riddle? Soon you'll see!

Intriguing maps, not needed naps, gazing over a waveless sea,
I could be a mouse or I could be a tree, who am I?
Friend, let's figure this out, just you and me,
I could be a NASCAR racer, *whoosh!* So fast!
Or maybe a historic person way back in the past.

Now it's the end of the poem, oh, you ask why?
Because, have you guessed yet, it's time to find out,
Who am I?

Answer: Me.

Jude Sharpe (10)
St Charles' Catholic Primary School, Hadfield

This Is Me!

The spider was a devil inching down the wall,
It was big and hairy and I didn't want to go near,
So I shouted for my mum as it started to crawl,
I ran upstairs with fear all over,
And I ran around like a Range Rover.

Like potatoes floating in the ocean, manatees relaxed in the ultramarine water,
I love marvellous manatees chilling underwater,
A life without manatees would be torture.

As my fish is swimming with eyes like golfballs,
The plants swayed in the water,
This fish makes my life a whole lot better,
And every day he puts a smile on my face.

Natalie Ann Rolls (10)
St Charles' Catholic Primary School, Hadfield

This Is Me

T he netball is a ball of shooting fire flying into the net,
H ershey's are my favourite chocolates out of Minstrels,
I hate cows as they stare at everyone with their beady eyes, like a staring contest,
S hopping for clothes, they're my friends as they want me to wear them all the time.

I love my family as they treat me all the time,
S unny days, snakes like to slither.

M usic is like a happy dream while I listen to good 4 u,
E veryone can play Pac-Man but we all have to take turns!

Béa Sues Amore Cassells (10)
St Charles' Catholic Primary School, Hadfield

This Is Me

If you want to know my biggest fears,
They are spiders and heights,
And as darkness walked into the room,
I am glad I found some light!

Like a gift from God,
The ice cream came down,
But when I looked at my sister,
She was jealous and had a big funny frown.

Holiday is heaven when you're enjoying it,
That's for sure,
I want to come here again,
And enjoy it once more.

The big bouncy bed is bound to be mine,
Look at it glow,
Look at it shine.

Amelia Boby (10)
St Charles' Catholic Primary School, Hadfield

This Is Me!

The spider, which was jogging down my wall, was as scary as a grizzly bear,
As fast as I could, I bolted out of the room before the spider could come near me!
Sam the spider crawled around the creepy house,
The spider sprinted across the wall as I was trying to catch it.

My dog sprinted across the park like a ball of light,
My dog barks as loud as a volcano when it erupts!
As far as I could, I threw my dog's toy across the park,
The dog who was enjoying his food was wagging his tail.

Evie Westmerland (10)
St Charles' Catholic Primary School, Hadfield

This Is Me!

I'm Maisey, don't call me lazy,
Oh and no I don't like daisies,
'Cause I'm as cool as Slim Shady,
So please stand up.

My favourite food is chicken nuggets,
From McDonald's, from McDonald's,
Like a magnet attracted to metal,
I'm obsessed with them, obsessed with them.

My bed is cosy,
And it smells like a posy,
It also smells like a rose,
And that's how my poem goes.

Maisey Mellor (10)
St Charles' Catholic Primary School, Hadfield

This Is Me!

The spider was a monster as it crawled up the wall,
I started to yell as it got closer,
The spider was huge and fuzzy,
So I ran around the room like a roller coaster!

My dog sat there,
Like a little teddy bear,
As I stroked its white, fluffy hair,
It barked as a man from the park walked by.

Last week,
I went to the beach,
I heard the waves crash and creep in,
As I threw my rubbish in the bin.

Rosie Thomasson (11)
St Charles' Catholic Primary School, Hadfield

This Is Me

Like a bolt of lightning, I kicked the ball across the net,
It went as high as a plane, that flew across the sea,
Then I came to Curzon, now that was a please,
Now this is about me.

Hi, my name is Thomas, and don't call me Tommy because it's not funny,
People say I'm crazy, but they are lazy,
So I love football, it's my thing, but the best thing is Sky Sports where football is live and you can see the price!

Thomas Doodson (10)
St Charles' Catholic Primary School, Hadfield

This Is Me

T he dogs are as fluffy as a teddy bear,
H orses are the cutest in the world,
I ce cream is my favourite, imagining it melting,
S piders are like monsters crawling down the wall.

I love dogs,
S nakes are scary as they slither around.

M y bed is as comfy as a cloud,
E gypt is my favourite holiday, imagining being on the beach.

Evie Aurora Littler (10)
St Charles' Catholic Primary School, Hadfield

This Is Me!

As I put a dot on my page,
The colour was beige.
I made a tree like a messed-up line,
And then I realised the time!

I went to McDonald's to get some fries,
But I ended up with a pie!
I wanted a rap,
But there was a tap.

The water was clear,
And I looked over the pair!
I drank it out of a cup,
And the water went up!

Mabel Mae Margaret Tymon (10)
St Charles' Catholic Primary School, Hadfield

This Is Me

T hursdays are the best,
H appy is the best feeling in the world,
I ce cream is like a dream,
S tomp! My dog stomped its foot.

I ce cubes, use Lego bricks,
S piders are fascinating.

M y most preferred sport is football,
E aster is the most celebrated thing in the world.

Tomos Wrigglesworth (10)
St Charles' Catholic Primary School, Hadfield

This Is Me

T he tacos screamed as I bit into them,
H olidays are my favourite,
I like to draw and dance,
S prouts are smelly.

I want to go to Spain,
S ummer days are the best.

M y cats are called Luna and Nova, they are very fast,
E www, snails are gross.

Jessica Bevins (10)
St Charles' Catholic Primary School, Hadfield

This Is Me!

T he dark is one of my biggest fears,
H enry is the laziest dog ever,
I have arachnophobia,
S t Charles' is the best school ever.

I swim gracefully like a dolphin,
S piders are demons.

M um and Dad are the best,
E xploring is fun!

Ruby Stilwell (10)
St Charles' Catholic Primary School, Hadfield

This Is Me!

  L orenzo is my name, and I love it,
  O n Monday we went to the park,
  R ico, my brother, argued with me,
"E at your dinner," said my mum,
"N o being mean to Milo," shouted my dad,
  Z oo animals are my favourite,
  O n Tuesday we went to the farm.

Lorenzo Sassanelli (10)
St Charles' Catholic Primary School, Hadfield

This Is Me!

T he football hurled into the net,
H olidays in Spain are the best,
I taly is a fantastic place to go to,
S pain is really cool.

I like Greece,
S pain is really hot.

M usic is the best,
E els are sticky and slimy.

Leon Groom (10)
St Charles' Catholic Primary School, Hadfield

What Act Am I?

It makes me feel all warm inside,
I like to help people if they are struggling,
When you do the opposite it can make someone upset,
My family gives me it like a tap gives you water,
A hug can secure it,
It fills in the gaps inside...
What act am I?

A: Kindness.

Lola Mills (10)
St Charles' Catholic Primary School, Hadfield

This Is Me!

Like Cinderella, I twirled around the room in my new party dress and sparkly shoes,
I was dancing with glee as my mum and dad took pictures of me,
As midnight struck, I ran upstairs to be tucked in below the stars.

Dancing is the best thing to do!

Ellie Owen (10)
St Charles' Catholic Primary School, Hadfield

This Is Me!

Black is my favourite colour,
My favourite thing is to read,
Courageous, kind and loving;
This is me!

My personality is one of a kind,
No one can buy it from me,
I am funny, kind and truthful;
This is me!

The animal I like lives in the woods,
It is brave, caring and protective.
I would act the same around my friends,
The animal I like is a wolf;
This is me!

At school my least favourite subject is RE,
My favourite is art,
Where I can explore my imagination and try to bring it alive;
This is me!

I am very obedient, I listen to my Mum,
We help her out sometimes and give her spas,
She is my favourite person, I will always love her;
This is me!

Family first, super-friends second, third is video games,
That is my rule and it is better than a cute poodle,
My personality is better than a boutique;
This is me!

My voice is booming loud, that makes me proud,
Unique, meek and sweet I am, I protect my siblings,
I am an example, giving away free samples,
Test me out and find my personality;
This is me!

Fast and furious, keen and curious,
Always making people happy,
Terrible memory, sometimes super scary,
Upsetting anything I love, my soul is no more a dove,

Now a wreckage, I don't like being sad, please apologise now;
This is me!

Sophia Varnava (10)
St Theresa's RC School, Finchley

Be You! Be Proud!

I'm a very special one, so very, very unique.
I don't have toes nor a nose, I don't even have a beak!
My hair grows fruit, it is very yummy.
I have rainbow skin!
But still no feathers, how very weird I am, *sigh*.
Mum tells me ablloogy, translated to be yourself.
Dad tells me aggongropaglu, translated to we're right behind you.
And they both say abblogruihgal cogulen ronp ronp pong yeee,
Translated to, be proud of who you are, your personality is like no other,
You're fun, caring, helpful, energetic, silly, cool, funny, happy, strong, brave,
You fight for what you believe in and you're great at lots of things,
Like art, fashion, baking, cooking, maths, drawing, programming, sport and watching TV, *haha!*
But remember you're the best you can be!
You're an alien!

Séamus Mac Crossan (10)
St Theresa's RC School, Finchley

How To Make An Extraordinary Evie!

A spoonful of courage and bravery,
And likes my sweet from savoury.
Family first,
Never burst.
This is me, extraordinary Evie!

A sprinkle of talent,
And a loving heart.
Always with a beaming smile,
And love running miles.
This is me, extraordinary Evie!

A brimmed bag full of pastel colours,
And always helping my mother.
I will never forget the day,
She saved my life.
This is me, extraordinary Evie!

A dollop of friends,
And my love never ends.

Sensible and careful,
And a blitz of compassion.
This is me, extraordinary Evie!

Silky and intelligent elephants,
Are my favourite animal.
I love sport and English,
And we can't forget to mix well for ten years to make an
Extraordinary Evie!
Made with pure love.

Evie Keating (10)
St Theresa's RC School, Finchley

This Is Me!

Orange, yellow, pink and blue,
Cats, pandas and a kangaroo,
I like all of these things,
These are the things that make me, me.

Blonde hair and light blue eyes,
I do not despise,
These are the things that make me unique,
Everything in my wardrobe's from a fabulous fashion boutique!

Kind, generous and bubbly,
With these personalities, I'm really lovely,
I can be funnier than everything,
But I'm not boasting or anything!

I'm the eldest sister of three,
And I act responsibly,
I set a great example,
Of all good things, I am a sample.

All of these things
Make me who I am,
I can only be proud of that,
This is me, Darcy!

Darcy O'Donnell (10)
St Theresa's RC School, Finchley

Me, Rio!

Sitting calm and content on a wooden bench,
Chatting and joking with friends.
Some family from France, yet speak little French,
My friendships will never end.

Love football and Arsenal,
Heroes are Smith-Rowe and Saka,
Also, add Auba and Laca.

Funny and loving,
Helpful and here to cheer all.
I try to be considerate,
While also being appreciable.

I have an older brother
Who makes me boil with anger,
And is very infuriating!

As I now sit down, calm and content on a wooden bench,
Chatting and joking with friends.

Some family from France, yet speak little French,
My friendships will never end.

This is me, Rio.

Rio Petnga Petnga-Wallace (10)
St Theresa's RC School, Finchley

This Is Me!

I'm loving, kind and strong,
Whenever I doubt myself my family always says I am wrong,
Positively I will always live,
But I will never be greedy and always give,
This is me!

I will always love,
And shine bright like a dove,
Even though I'm an only child,
I will always be seen with a smile,
This is me!

I love all races,
And all faces,
I adore God,
And I have never touched a fishing rod,
This is me!

I like to sing,
Even if it is not my thing,
Bing, bang, bong,
This poem wasn't very long,

For my dog I defend,
Now this is the end,
This is me!
Olivia.

Olivia Dina (10)
St Theresa's RC School, Finchley

Me

Amazing and kind
Courageous and colourful
My mum, my dad and my sister
Are all my inspiration
This is Mamie
This is me!
Bees buzzing and monkeys dancing
Hot chocolate, onesies and warm woollen mittens
Slippers, dressing gowns and cuddles
Homemade meals straight from the oven
This is Mamie
This is me!
A dash of bravery
A spoonful of love
A bucket of intelligence
All the colours of the rainbow
This is Mamie
This is me!
An astronaut is what I want to be
No fireman
No teacher, no!

I want to be in NASA
This is Mamie
This is me!
And I am never going to change.

Mamie Crossan (10)
St Theresa's RC School, Finchley

Michal Madness

Hi, my name is Michal
I have a younger brother
Please don't make me stutter
Or I will tell my mother.

My hero is Rick Peacock-Edwards
He was a fave flyer
I'll be a better flyer
As long as I don't catch fire.

I originate from Poland
Of this I am proud
But my voice is sometimes
Booming and loud.

I am very tall
I just hope I won't fall
I have a lot of friends
We sometimes shout like hens.

I love my family very much
We are a terrific bunch

These are my closing remarks
This is me
I am Michal.

Michal Rojek (10)
St Theresa's RC School, Finchley

How To Create A Phenomenal And Perfect Lena (Baked With Love And Care)

1. Start with a bag of bravery and courageousness.
2. Pour in a litre of positivity.
3. Gently sprinkle in some artistic talent.
4. Pour in a tablespoon of humour.
5. While mixing, sprinkle in anime with your fingers.
6. Pour in five tablespoons of loyalty.
7. Mix everything together.
8. Place carefully in the oven.
9. After waiting for five minutes, squeeze Sagittarius frosting carefully on top, around in circles.

Voila! Your dream friend is created. Enjoy! Remember, never add a tablespoon of anger, and treat your friend nicely.

Lena Rapala (10)
St Theresa's RC School, Finchley

This Is Me!

Violet, aqua and cream,
Colours that are sure to make you scream,
A doctor or a baker is what I dream to be,
This is me!

My mum, my dad and my family,
All kind and compassionate,
Keeping me safe with somewhere to stay,
This is me!

Doodling and drawing is what I like to do,
Pineapple's my favourite fruit,
Cherries and strawberries too,
Ice cream on a summer's day,
This is me!

Having a blast with all my friends,
Together our friendship will never end,
This is me!

Tanisha Chowdhury (10)
St Theresa's RC School, Finchley

Connor's Favourites

My favourite god is Apollo.
I used to like trees hollow.
I love Marvel, my favourite superhero is Spider-Man.
It's obvious that snow leopards rule, but Bart Simpson is a fool.
But still my favourite.
This is me!

I am Italian, I wish I had a stallion.
Gaming is my thing and I wish I had wings.
I hate tomatoes and dropslides
Dropslides are too scary, why, why, why!
Love Lego, listen to what I say because it looks awesome at the end.
And...

This is me!
Connor.

Connor Balestrini (10)
St Theresa's RC School, Finchley

This Is Me!

Indigo, sage green, yellow,
Always kind, loving and mellow,
Dreams for the future,
A doctor or interior designer,
Here I come,
I will be one!
This is me!

Darcy, Evie, Olivia,
My great friends,
Our friendship will never end!
A big sister to keep me safe,
A loving mother to embrace,
This is me!

Sushi, popcorn, strawberries,
Hamsters, axolotls, bunnies,
My favourite things,
Swimming, maths, English,
My hobbies!
This is me!
Isabel.

Isabel Luz Martins (10)
St Theresa's RC School, Finchley

How To Create A Scrumptious Bunch Of Bens

Grab a spoonful of courage and a pinch of delight, then mix it together with all of your might.
Pour the love into a sprinkle of smiles, then place it in an oven and leave it a while.
Fry up the humour, make sure the lumps are thick, then sieve it slowly and speed it up quick.
Finally, mix it all together and tie it up in a knot, then throw it in the air and into a pot.
Now you have created a scrumptious bunch of Bens, go out of your house and tell all of your friends.

Ben Blendis (10)
St Theresa's RC School, Finchley

How To Make A Plateful of Fatimas

1. Add a whole bag of love and kindness
2. A spoonful of bravery and a lot of courage
3. Sprinkle in some talent and smartness
4. And with that a dash of humour and laughter
5. A litre or two of unfailing loyalty
6. Add a spoon of anime
7. Now mix, mix, mix
8. Don't forget the rainbow sprinkles
9. Place in the oven for twenty minutes

Ta-da! Your perfect plateful of Fatimas.

Enjoy!

Fatima Mohamad (11)
St Theresa's RC School, Finchley

How To Make An Aryo

A spoonful of courage and a handful of love
Some sprinkles of smiles and peacefulness of a dove
Gently stir together and you have a piece.

One litre of positivity, kindness and compassion
My glasses are the form of high fashion
And a bowl of Iran which is half of me.

Pour in a younger brother who loves acting
Put in a cup of joyful laughter
Finally, a dollop of my favourite animal, penguin.

Aryo Khoshkam (10)
St Theresa's RC School, Finchley

Marvellous Me!

A beautiful, bright girl
A smile as big as the sea
She has blue-green eyes and they really shine
Dark blonde hair and she is very fair
Courageous and kind
Her favourite colour is purple
Her hobbies are swimming and baking
Her family and friends are the best
She is Latvian
And is ten
Her favourite animal is a penguin
There is still much more to learn
So come on and join the fun!

Margaret Rimsa (10)
St Theresa's RC School, Finchley

This Is Me!

I am a curious little boy
I love animals, especially big cats like lions and tigers
I also try extreme stuff like zip lining and climbing
I also am interested in nature stuff
I am always joyful
You don't want to mess with me because I am as fierce as a roaring tiger
I also have beautiful hazel eyes that look like a green field full of plants.
This is me!

Mikolaj Ceremuga (9)
St Theresa's RC School, Finchley

How To Make An Extraordinary Me

Add some kindness with a spoonful of joy,
With a pinch of love,
Pour in some courage and bravery,
But don't forget to water it down with sadness,
Sprinkle in some laughter and smiles,
Mix well while adding some peace, quiet and calm,
Put it in the oven and heat with anger,
Take it out and leave it to cool down,
And now you have got me!

Govind Hariharadas (10)
St Theresa's RC School, Finchley

This Is Me!

Hi, I'm lovely Lily
This is a poem about me
I'm very tall like a giraffe
I can jump really high
I'm kind when I'm calm
I am curious about my mum's conversations
When I'm stressed I get depressed
I like to be adventurous
I like to find gold
When I'm mad I get sad
This is me!

Lily Losi (8)
St Theresa's RC School, Finchley

This Is Me!

I am the wind, swift and light
Like an ant I am small but smart
I am Alice in Wonderland, curious and brave
I am a bookworm consuming books with my eyes
I am an animal lover
My hair is melted chocolate
My eyes are as black as diamonds
Roses are red
Violets are blue
This poem is about me
Not you!

Shirley Suet Ling Chan (9)
St Theresa's RC School, Finchley

This Is Me!

J oyful and funny, the best younger brother, calm and quiet, a big social life,
A dd a spoonful of courage, setting an example for the younger ones,
G reen, blue and yellow, opaque and quite mellow, I like everyone regardless,
O veractive and always direct, never too slow, always catching up with others.

Jago Hartnett (10)
St Theresa's RC School, Finchley

Chimdi

Purple, pink and blue
Perky pandas, fluffy rabbits
A love for drawing
This is me.

Friendly, loving and kind
Always with a beaming smile
Trusting and thoughtful
This is me.

A big sister to Chlamaka and Chisom
A helpful daughter
An amazing student
This is me.

Chimdi Ekezie (11)
St Theresa's RC School, Finchley

This Is Me!

Hi, my name is Arvin
I am as fast as a cheetah
My favourite thing is building Lego because it makes me smart
My favourite subject is maths
I am smart and sincere
My dream is to build a business centre
The thing that makes me happy when I am sad is hearing music
I am as hungry as a lion.

Arvin
St Theresa's RC School, Finchley

This Is Me!

I am a magician, waving my brush while I paint,
I am short but intelligent,
I work as quick as a computer,
My mind twists in adventures,
I chill in my bed, under my covers,
I am a mouse in the loud house,
I love to help others in need,
My hair is as silky as chocolate,
This is me!

Aleksandra Deda (9)
St Theresa's RC School, Finchley

My Favourite Game

FIFA 22 is my favourite game
It reminds me of how much I love football
Scoring goals is my priority
But my sweet spot is dribbling
It is the best
But the actual best thing is the summer fest
Griezmann, Mbappé and the whole French squad
They all make appearances on the quad.

Lucas Lazarevic (9)
St Theresa's RC School, Finchley

How To Make A Batch Of Luke

All you need is:
A spoonful of courage and determination,
Add a bag of bravery,
Then some bits of tasty football,
Don't forget a pencil and paper,
Also lots of yummy, funny humour,
Then a litre of Arsenal,
Bake for a few minutes,
You've just created a batch of Luke!

Luke Hare (10)
St Theresa's RC School, Finchley

My Favourite Animal

He is amphibious,
He loves a swim,
He mostly sleeps,
Twenty-three hours a day,
He loves to play,
An hour a day,
He will hang from branches,
And climb at glacial speed,
I like him and he likes me!
I bet you can't guess who it is.

Answer: Sloth.

Euan Kirby (10)
St Theresa's RC School, Finchley

What I Love And Who I Am

I am a hero on the pitch,
I am an excellent, caring brother,
I am a pro at piano,
The colour red stands for Arsenal,
My family is the best family I could ever have,
I couldn't wish for more,
Arsenal is the home of football,
I am the best me I could ever be!

Nathan Gulati (9)
St Theresa's RC School, Finchley

This Is Me

- **T** here are different feelings
- **H** owever, it depends
- **I** t may be happy or sad
- **S** ometimes frustrated or surprised.

- **I** am a giant
- **S** tomping around.

- **M** e helping others
- **E** lizabeth I am, and always will be.

Elizabeth Muci (9)
St Theresa's RC School, Finchley

This Is Me!

I am as chilled as a sofa
I am as sporty as a football pitch
My eyes are as green as a pea
I am as angry as Shrek
I do not like carrots
I am as sweet as a milkshake
I am as smart as Einstein
My hair is as bright as the sun
This is me!

Evie Boverhoff (9)
St Theresa's RC School, Finchley

This Is Me!

I am like a classical band
I am adventurous but clumsy
I am as silly as a baby
I am fearless but loving
I am as messy as a pig
I am as weird as a blobfish
My hair is like a piece of gum stuck
My eyes are dark chocolate.
This is me!

Christina Romanova
St Theresa's RC School, Finchley

Lily's Bake

A spoonful of animals and colour.
A cupful of adventure and creativity.
A sprinkle of fun and laughter.
A blitz of compassion.
Mix well with sign language and Makaton.
A dash of chocolate to colour my eyes.
Bake for ten years until perfect.

Lily Farrugia (10)
St Theresa's RC School, Finchley

This Is Me!

I am adventurous like a monkey swinging on trees.
I am brave like a roaring lion.
I am curious like a scientist.
My hair is brown like milk chocolate.
My hair is wavy as a wave
My eyes are as dark as dark chocolate
My name is Amazing Alice.

Alice Mariam Subin (8)
St Theresa's RC School, Finchley

Who I Am

A mazing, great, courageous and sporty
L oving, respectful, peaceful and successful
P eaceful, helpful, joyful and playful
H opeful, faithful, I am the most loyal
Y oung, brave and honest, this is me.

Alphy!

Alphy Mubiru (11)
St Theresa's RC School, Finchley

This Is Me!

I am very small but great at basketball
My dream is to be a basketball player
But my dad says I'm too small
I'm like a parrot on the concert stage
My hair is as red as a rose
I have a younger sister and an older sister
This is me.

Erin
St Theresa's RC School, Finchley

This Is Me!

I am as happy as a baby chick
My hair is as soft as silk
My eyes are as green as nature
I am tall but I can reach all of the high things
I am as smart as a scientist
I like energetic dogs and ostriches
I am as excited as a baby dog.

Gabriella Broom (8)
St Theresa's RC School, Finchley

This Is Me!

I am a lover of animals
My hair is as wavy as the sea
My eyes are as green as nature
My hair is as blonde as the sand
I love bunnies
I love dogs
I love music
I love singing like Ariana Grande.
This is me!

Oliwia Weiss (8)
St Theresa's RC School, Finchley

This Is Me!

I am as friendly as can be
I am kind, I also have a very big mind
I am as polite as a friend
I love animals as much as my parents
My hair is milk chocolate
And my eyes are blue
I am a swan on stage
This is me!

Kristiana Grozdanova (8)
St Theresa's RC School, Finchley

Jordan The Great

J ordan is amazing.
O verfilled with kindness.
R unning to school.
D aniel is my best friend.
A nd I am ten years old.
N o, I don't have a sister, I have only one brother.

Jordan Argiev (10)
St Theresa's RC School, Finchley

This Is How To Make A Dom

Now a spoonful of football.
Now a spoonful of kindness.
Something that's called courage.
A sprinkle of some coolness.
Let's add bravery.
Wait, we forgot some loyalness.
By the way, I am the best.

Dominykas Sapka (10)
St Theresa's RC School, Finchley

My Dog Maggie

She's really kind, but she is cheeky,
Just sometimes,
I really love her because she's so cute,
If you don't like her then you're just unreal,
She has floppy ears and ginger fur,
This is me!

Sofia Morozova (9)
St Theresa's RC School, Finchley

Flaming Madness

I am a master at gaming
I am as silly as a duck
My hair is as black as a polar bear
I sometimes get too angry like a flaming dart
I am a lion strong and brave
I can make other people flame.

Brendan Amponsah (8)
St Theresa's RC School, Finchley

My Favourite Game

The logo is red
I play it in bed
All my friends play it
I wish I could name it!
I wonder why it was made
But it helps me like a first aid!
Let me be!

This is me!

Imina Osaren (9)
St Theresa's RC School, Finchley

All About Me

I am as strong as a panther
I am as angry as a lion
I am as brutal as a bear
I am as bold as a fighter
I am as sporty as a sportsman
I miss my brother.

This is me!

Nathaniel Asare Yiadom (8)
St Theresa's RC School, Finchley

I'm Me!

Hi, I'm Manuela,
I'm from Brazil,
I love to sing,
I'm pretty small,
My Zodiac sign is Capricorn,
I love to help.

I'm me!

Manuela Maglione (9)
St Theresa's RC School, Finchley

All About Me!

Football is my life.
How could I lose it?
It is my thing.
So what could I do?

Tanks are the best.
They can go west.
In the nest.

Nea Gibson (9)
St Theresa's RC School, Finchley

Toys

T eddy, clean and special
O ld and new, I like to be with you
Y ou are my soft teddy
S ix teddies in the box.

Gabriela Suarez (5)
St Theresa's RC School, Finchley

Toys

T wo bears at the fair
O ne octopus at the park
Y o-yos and a jack-in-the-box
S ix snakes and soft toys.

Katy Boverhoff (5)
St Theresa's RC School, Finchley

Toys

T oys I love
O ctopus floating
Y o-yo bouncing
S nake slithering.

Max S Szymanski (5)
St Theresa's RC School, Finchley

Toys

T eddy in the park
O ctopus too
Y ellow unicorn
S hiny and new.

Taybah Chowdhury (5)
St Theresa's RC School, Finchley

Toys

T oys
O pen the box
Y o-yo, yo-yo
S lithery snake.

Ted Blendis (5)
St Theresa's RC School, Finchley

Toys

T eddy is new
O pen my box
Y ou jump up
S o soft.

Elzana Dereje (5)
St Theresa's RC School, Finchley

To Create Me You Will Need

Sugar for my sweetness
A bowlful of long hair
Some paint for my creativeness
Last of all, a Lailah and an Esmai because they are my best friends.

First, you will need to put the sugar in.
Then, you need to add the paint and long hair and give it a stir.
Finally, throw in the Lailah and Esmai.
Blend it all together, and enjoy!

Honor Anderson (8)
Weavervale Primary School, Frodsham

To Make A Sakhe Cake

A splash of kindness and a few angry sprinkles.
Some grapes and some sugar, and a lot of TV.
Some hand sanitiser and lots of food!
Style and lots of sweets.
Craziness and cash, cash, cash!
Xbox and electronics.
Put it all in the oven and you get a yummy Sakhe cake!
Oh, don't forget the KFC.

Sakhe Ntombela (7)
Weavervale Primary School, Frodsham

This Person Is...

A girl
And when she eats pasta she gets it all over her face
I think it's quite funny
And she loves truth or dare
And she's very friendly
Oh, and don't forget she likes Chinese
Oh, and I'm not done
She wants to be an artist when she grows up.

Charlotte Daniels (8)
Weavervale Primary School, Frodsham

Tilly And Elsa

Tilly and Elsa are my cats,
I like them much more than I like bats.
Elsa is black and white whilst
Tilly is grey and white.
I wish they were pink and purple.
My cats are my favourite thing in the world,
I like it when their tails are curled.

Emeliá-Rose Ellis (7)
Weavervale Primary School, Frodsham

This Is Me

I'm a gamer, I'm a player
I'm sour, depending on the hour
I get mad for a short while
And maths is my calm place
When I get mad and I get sour
And I'm extremely intelligent
And my favourite pet is an axolotl.

Noah Winter (8)
Weavervale Primary School, Frodsham

My Emotions Everyday!

On Monday I am mad
On Tuesday I am sad
On Wednesday I am tired
On Thursday I am mithered
On Friday I am yappy
On Saturday I am happy
And on Sunday I am... cheeky!
Then all together I am... crazy Daisy!

Daisy Wilson (8)
Weavervale Primary School, Frodsham

Harriet

H appy as Miss Baker in a sweet shop
A lways playing football
R eally funny
R eally friendly
I love to eat cake
E xtremely blonde and blue-eyed
T hat is me!

Harriet Hill (7)
Weavervale Primary School, Frodsham

How To Make Lucas

A book-filled bedroom.
A spoonful of fun and mischief.
A pinch of cheekiness.
A dash of brightness.
A sprinkle of happiness.
A slab of hot cheesy pizza.
Slice, and that is how you make a Lucas!

Lucas Cross (8)
Weavervale Primary School, Frodsham

The Ingredients You Need To Make Terrific Thomas

A dip of games
A sprinkle of YouTube
Forty lorries of Minecraft and Trailmakers
A drop of coke
Then put me in the freezer, not the oven!
Thomas doesn't like heat.

Thomas Fairfield (8)
Weavervale Primary School, Frodsham

Esmai

E xcellent at doing anything!
S pecial because of my eyes!
M agnificent at maths!
A nimal lover of cats.
I ncredible at handwriting.

Esmai Leicester (7)
Weavervale Primary School, Frodsham

Matthew

My favourite animal can bite and he's tiny.
He is cute with light brown and white fur.
He has big floppy ears.
He eats and drinks from a bowl.
What is he?

Matthew Green (8)
Weavervale Primary School, Frodsham

What Am I?

My favourite animal hoots at night,
But not when it's light.
It eats mice and sleeps when it's light,
But stays awake in the night.
What am I?

Lailah Winter (7)
Weavervale Primary School, Frodsham

Harley

On Sunday I am mad
On Friday I am happy
On Thursday okay
On Monday I'm tired
On Saturday I'm good
Tuesday I'm crazy.

Harley Mawdsley (7)
Weavervale Primary School, Frodsham

YoungWriters Est. 1991

YOUNG WRITERS INFORMATION

We hope you have enjoyed reading this book – and that you will continue to in the coming years.

If you're the parent or family member of an enthusiastic poet or story writer, do visit our website **www.youngwriters.co.uk/subscribe** and sign up to receive news, competitions, writing challenges and tips, activities and much, much more! There's lots to keep budding writers motivated!

If you would like to order further copies of this book, or any of our other titles, then please give us a call or order via your online account.

Young Writers
Remus House
Coltsfoot Drive
Peterborough
PE2 9BF
(01733) 890066
info@youngwriters.co.uk

Join in the conversation!
Tips, news, giveaways and much more!

🅕 YoungWritersUK   🅧 YoungWritersCW   📷 youngwriterscw